Solus Urger Voyager

David Groulx

Copyright © 2023 by David Groulx

All rights reserved. No part of this publication may be reproduced or transmitted in any form or by any means, electronic or mechanical, including photocopying, recording or any information storage and retrieval, without the written permission of the publisher. Names, characters, places and incidents are either the product of the author's imagination or used fictitiously, and any resemblance to actual persons living or dead, events or locales is entirely coincidental. All trademarks are properties of their respective owners.

Published by
BookLand Press Inc.
15 Allstate Parkway
Suite 600
Markham, Ontario L3R 5B4
www.booklandpress.com

Printed in Canada

Front cover image by Depositphotos

Library and Archives Canada Cataloguing in Publication

Title: Solus urger voyager / David Groulx.
Names: Groulx, David, 1969- author.
Description: Series statement: Modern Indigenous voices
Identifiers: Canadiana (print) 20230182526 | Canadiana (ebook) 20230182534 | ISBN 9781772312089 (softcover) |
ISBN 9781772312096 (EPUB)
Subjects: LCGFT: Poetry.
Classification: LCC PS8563.R76 S65 2023 | DDC C811/.54—dc23

We acknowledge the support of the Government of Canada through the Canada Book Fund and the support of the Ontario Arts Council, an agency of the Government of Ontario. We also acknowledge the support of the Canada Council for the Arts.

Solus Urger Voyager

Table of Contents

A left | 9

A bow | 11

A thought | 12

A stolen dog | 13

An old man sits | 14

Still on bed | 15

A dog chases a rabbit | 16

An old man says | 17

Hands were made callous here | 19

Two tornados | 20

A laying of hands | 21

These poems are my bullets | 22

A wolf's tooth on my head | 23

Jesus could not have walked on our water | 24

I am skin too | 25

A new house, new paint | 26

I am an unbound river | 27

Geese fly over you | 28

Dear June | 29

The master's tools | 30

Grandfathers | 31

I say good morning | 32

Available dog | 33

Lived/unlived | 34

A breaking open of the belly | 35

Feral sin | 40

Market value of butchery | 41

Come to believe | 42

A short study of settler | 43

Charity | 44

Notes on living | 45

Dear Python, god of the pit | 46

Passing oblivion | 47

Oh your age | 48

Let's talk…ring…ring | 49

Just doing it | 50

While you were in the other room watching TV | 51

Why poems are like x's | 52

Pandemic TV watching | 53

Trip to the dump | 54

While I'm here | 55

The dead god goes camping | 56

Muse's standard contract(s) | 57

Margaret Atwood's library | 58

Whatever a Killdeer stands up to see | 59

Cygnus punch | 60

The Douglas, Walt Whitman circa 1967 | 61

Always propagandas | 62

A left

I am left

I am all that's left,

left

swept up

what's left?

human excrement,

left

hate us

clean toilets

for university students

make the bricks for court houses

lawyers

argue about how

clean the window ought to be.

Who can afford books?

goes home.

The bookmobile

turns left into my neighbourhood

every 2nd Saturday of the month.

A bow

My neck was always a bow. As

a child I

broke it,

"Daddy," I said, one day while coming out of the water,

"I think I've broken my neck"

He said,

"autumn children always come

when a marriage is broken."

I slept for weeks

sitting up,

hoping I was an owl.

A thought

I remember the ice on the lake behind our house,

winter

freezing like iron cracking.

Our house was a highway,

moaning in the cold,

life moved, but

you had to shiver to feel it.

A stolen dog

I have been known to steal bread

because of hunger.

fire wood

to keep warm.

other people's dogs

for company.

the rest, I worked

for.

An old man sits

There is an old man

sitting alone

like God

and

every morning on my way

to work. He's there

This morning there is an

old woman

sitting with him.

I am happy he's not alone.

Still on bed

I lay still on my bed

monster was underneath,

poking out its penis

from under the bed.

Don't cry,

endure,

you suffer you

count the years

it takes,

feel human again.

You

share

this with

no...

monster underneath.

A dog chases a rabbit

A dog chases rabbit

rabbit dictates chase

dog follows argument

about life and death

the rabbit stops.

The universe is insensitive to our

plight Mr. Dog.

Our lives, lived under the siege of daylight

and the night time.

The Dog, being philosophical about it,

breaks rabbit's neck

Yes, says dog

We are pillaged by the seasons,

blood dripping off its snout.

An old man says

Now you work
old man says

now you put your shoulder to the day
no slouching
no dog fucking
the old man says

earn your pay
seize the morning with your bare hands
put your back into it!
old man says

You wanted to drink like a man last night
now you work like a man
old man says

noise and the racket begin
machines billowing smoke & dust
men yelling for more hot
young boys scratching gravel
like mules
day light is burning!
old man says

Amen! danse macabre
their mops over rolling felt
yelling 'the soup is too cold!'
pot man cranks up his burners
there is nothing but the sound of the kettle rumbling
nothing but the smell of hot tar burning
roof begins to vibrate

old man smiles
his opera
his magnum opus.

Hands were made callous here

Before these mountains were torn off the earth

Before these rivers ran red earth with her blood

Men made their hands callous here

Men heaved the bone-earth for bread

Men made a town here once

with their fists and shoulders,

that kind of poetry that is

written with sweat and a knowing of death

few would know.

Here we made our hands callous

with hope.

Here we dug our graves

for our fathers.

Two tornados

There were two tornados in our home,

one was my mother

one was my father.

My father on the second floor

My mother on the first

I hid in the cellar

holding a weathervane.

A laying of hands

When I was a boy, I was deaf in one ear,

my mother would take me to tent revivals

on Manitoulin Island.

A congregation,

rousing that furious rage

that only God

could hear.

These poems are my bullets

These poems are my bullets
Tell the settler
To take his gold with him, wherever it melts
These poems are my bullets
to get what is owed, what is due
This pen is my gun, drawing a bead

You see these poems are my bullets

My mother went to your schools
where she was taught to hate herself
and taught it to my sisters and I

These poems are my bullets you see
I have hunted many four-legged
but this is the first time I have ever killed a
man with a poem.

A wolf's tooth on my head

The lungs of the earth
piled in a heap,

gasps,

and the wisp that

is life

is going out.

Jesus could not have walked on our water

Jesus could not have walked on our water,
water belongs to Mishipishu[1]

Jesus couldn't have flown into this sky,
sky belongs to Thunderbird[2]

You see, settler, you see occupier, you see colonizer?
You see settler, you see occupier, you see colonizer?

This land was created by one breath
all of creation,
one dead little muskrat, a little mud
in its paw.

---

[1] *Mishipishu* - Ojibwa mythological spirit.
[2] *Thunderbird* - Ojibwa mythological spirit.

I am skin too

My brothers fill the mow of
your prisons
I myself have been there.

Our children fill your foster homes
I myself have been there too.

My people fill your graveyards
one day I myself will be there too.

A new house, new paint

On my grandfather's new house we
painted a Thunderbird
it was his power

We painted Thunderbird
on his house
because he is our ancestor

I am an unbound river

I am
two people, two halves
made whole

two separate lives

roaring

I am other to you
I am other to them

fixed pieces scattered

I am deep
I am wide
I am moving
I am sacred

I have one tongue

can you undo it for me?

Geese fly over you

Rain must be danced
sun must be danced
touch the ground

do not turn away
do not go blind
do not look down Nanabush[1]

grass must be sung
tress must be sung

do not turn away
do not go blind
do not look down Nanabush[1]

earth is looking up at you
rain will come

---

[1]*Nanabush* - Ojibwa Trickster

Dear June

Dear June

I did go to Jackson
I did mess around
I did teach all those women what they
didn't know how
people did stoop and bow

no, June they didn't lead me around
like a wounded hound
it's tail between its legs.

You see June,
there comes a time in every man's life
he must go to Jackson

when he must turn loose
play his hand, turn loose his coat.

Dear June
Goodbye Dear June.

The master's tools

I will not use the master's tools
to build the master's house

My throat will have bruises
from singing.

I will shift sounds and walls,
of the Master's language
I will take tobacco can lids
make jingles,

women can dance
sound can heal.

Grandfathers

are of the earth and
speaks of the nations

The Elk nation, the Moose nation, the Skunk nation, the Bass nation, the Blue jay nation, the Loon nation, the Puma nation, The Grouse nation. The River nation, the Lake nation. And all the other nations around here.

The nature of this earth

speaks through stone.

I say good morning

because, night has arms
reaching the moors of starlight,
leg muscles of a marathon runner
its memory, colour of vantablack
its heartbeats, lull
and
it is long
and I missed you.

Available dog

I drag a mangy available dog with me,
me and my available dog sit in the burned out ruins
of my basement
full of the stink of the rotting sins of congregations
left behind,
falling through the floor.
We play cards there.
He says, the history of sin is the history of man.
Dogs have never sinned
We have always been.
As another prisoner falls through the floor,
candle wax dripping through the floor.
I have two aces,
and from beneath his paw
available dog
pulls out deuces.

Lived/unlived

In this, there is the lived and unlived
you are the unlived, I am the lived.
You are the unlived and what is unlived
never shut's its mouth.

Noise noise noise.

What is unlived organizes its madness
by numbers. What is unlived forgets
the archive of my mouth,
the database that is my songs, the index
that is memories.

What is unlived is unbound and what is
lived, gathered and bound, unlived.

What is unlived goes into fits with its
words about what is unsaid because
I am unsaid, unlived, I am unsaid.

A breaking open of the belly

We are still here Aime, us the
niggers of the north
An otherness- nothingness imprisoned in our minds
by our colour

I have heard
of white writers who claim to be bush niggers
they live outside the high prison
walls
they are loved there
I have heard

and in here, they complain about the smell

We are still wretched Franz
red is our colour the revolution that was promised
has been broken over our shoulders
despised like heathen refugeeso
this country does not love us
It loves its idea of us
it gawks
it quakes

With its fuckin TV cameras
it rolls over us with its Hollywood
like scab ravaged lepers
they can't stand the smell
us, the scum of the earth, our knees
and hands digging into the earth
and the priest scum on our brown asses

There was a blue butterfly
that landed on my finger
That told me the history of our mountains long past
how he had escaped the jaws of a wasp
You say I am only part butterfly and part
gravel scratcher
All shudder
a woman's life is not worth very much
here Róża
They are not the colour of the
blue Madonna but the brown one

The dirt road does not die here
Róża
they are drowning us in the rivers
we, the grave diggers

I have an idea about you
You are the new Jerusalem and the
old testimony
of a god that died and lived again, returning
from death with nothing
of the sacred earth in his hands
and the only thing
that can fill the holes in his hands are coins
not sacred earth
Not so sacred is it?

We adore our drunken poets that eat lilacs
and vomit out eulogies to us, the dammed
Our darling girls contorted on the sidewalks
like preying mantis
The government hates them for
not paying taxes on the heads they eat
The politicians will tell us that it is public morality
headless, heartless shits

This new Jerusalem will have a wall, an idea
about me, a wall built with a tongue wagging
and ideology about reason and peace
and yet knowing nothing about them
or me, but prayers to a god that can read,
written on paper wrapped around a *Brimstone* missile
sent flying to brown and black people

They will understand god has chosen Rome to speak for him,
they will understand limbs torn off
they will understand the voice of god
they will understand the misery of god
they will understand markets

Coil the rising around me,
coil your habitual raving madness
coil around me the quenching of your thirsting
A heartbeat stretched over my broken ear
Come with me in the crippled dawn,
the sunlight will twist our shadows
and muzzle the darkness
Let me show you what has been destroyed in me
The wounds it has left
the bones it has broken
the beatings I have taken
till I awoke, exhausted
digging up words from the darkness
till my hands were bleeding

Her I am, your mongrel moon
your mutt of midnight
your dangerous memories
your rising nigger

Come with me now
this blessing is short
and we must hurry
till I must return to the beast that first
brought me to you

that cut the soul from the spirit
from the body from the spirit of the earth
What a sharp tongue you have grandmother
splitting and spitting up this fine Indian country

The nuns French kissed me and bit off
my tongue
Now with the land, on my side, my tongue
grows back
and I challenge them to do it again

What you think is dead is not dead
what you think is empty is not empty

Can you hear it
like a rat singing in that garbage heap
called Golgotha
they find our bodies in the river
pull them out and say its just Indians
put them there with the rest
and everybody pulled out is a failure
of a just society because... because
we were just Indians

Feral sin

I saw in you

a wild place

a feral urge

a holiness

you and I

we are damned

sacred

but damned.

Market value of butchery

They built a town next to our reservation
after a treaty was signed,
history said the town was built on the lumber industry

I said it was built on lies,
deceit and the butchering of a forest

The bush half eaten
left wounded
was the name of our reserve

Come to believe

I've come to believe

That sobriety is beneath me (or it's the floor)

That drunkenness is the highest form of consciousness

That love, indeed "stinks" (re: j geils band-thx)

That poetry requires the utmost commitment

That friends a hard to find

That my heart and my head will never agree on anything

That work and sex are both good for the soul

That people prefer pictures of wolves to the real thing (like everything natural)

That if the best things in life a free,
the worst things are paid for dearly

A short study of settler

They studied the life spans of people who sat

of people who stood

studied pavement in the winter

pavement in the summer

studied the sun the moon

stars

studied maggots

how women have orgasms

studied men's penises

studied the dust on coffee tables and coffee

the hearts of the broken hearted
studied the cries of newborn babies and why old men fart

studied happiness and sadness

the second lives of snails.

They forgot how to sing to water,

or they never knew.

Charity

Every holiday season I get an envelope from the War Amps.
Its for a donation
in case you lose your keys, they can be returned to you

I stare at it and think of the little children so brave
missing an arm or a leg
so tough,
brave.

Then I throw the envelope in the waste basket
and don't think about them anymore.

Notes on living

They say the smartest you will ever be is the day you are born inferring the dumbest you'll ever be is the day you die leaving you to wonder; what your best day will be?

always saying when this happens
it'll be my best day, when that happens
it'll be my best day and everyday
nothing happens, life's little
things happen and
moves on

you are a bird
left dead in the fence

stained red
marked memory like a scar
living like that
can only be human

Dear Python, god of the pit

One day I imagine the ghosts in my head will let me answer when they say, where have you been all of our lives? and I'll say had you been listening I'd have spoken sooner and we wouldn't have had to waste all of our lives just getting here. I could have been in the shower with the woman I love or in the kitchen cooking a red sauce and getting soused, I could have been watching a movie instead of here, whispering this poem from the deep.

Passing oblivion

Every autumn

I become existentialist, watch trees

bright orange, red, yellow

turning to bone death

ashen   empty   absurd

Oh your age

Time and money are an illusion, stay as human as you can.
What makes you afraid of death, is the illusion of time.

Anger twists the truth, rage is a route to madness.
The Serpent was beautiful, your motivations are not illusions.

Understand the moment you live in, your dog does.
Some of us have no illusions, we live beneath them.

The iron in our veins is broken star blood.
and poets are failures as people.

Let's talk…ring…ring

The boss that is inside my head

never sleeps

the boss that is inside my head

speaks only saga

the boss that is inside my head

has murdered the Iliad

the boss inside my head

is the reason suicide is not a solitary act

the boss inside my head

is the reason suicide is

not about murdering me

it's about murdering him.

Just doing it

If I had no other way to write,
but to be haunted in a lonely faraway place
I would do it

If I had to write myself
crazy till I wrote myself madness
I would do it

If I had to cut my fingers off
to write on my skin with my blood
I would do it

If I had to cut off your fingers
to write on your skin with your blood
I would do it

While you were in the other room watching TV

This morning

I woke up not loving you

it was raining

you were in the other room watching TV

and it was raining

I felt confined by it

and I began to love you again

the rain, all broken like

it always is

began to look wet

the sound of it fell against my ears

and I fell asleep again

while you were in the other room watching TV

Why poems are like x's

Go away little poem

go get published,

go shredded through a wire.

Go away little poem

go get gathered again,

you are whole without me.

Don't come back poem

I can't fix you.

Pandemic TV watching

There is a woman on TV
says she's God

I thinks she's a drunk
and her husband keeps her that way

cause she's easier to deal with
in some
twisted act of faith.

A monk to her delusion.
I
to mine.
You
to yours.

Trip to the dump

I used to live with a woman who collected photographs
of people she knew

years later, when she left

she didn't even want the photographs she had
of us,

memories are not
black & white, she said

not to be lugged around,

so I took them to the dump

and the guy charged me 20$ to dump them

something about polluting the environment

which seemed kind of odd to me

and after I paid the guy

I had 20$ less to lug around

which didn't explain any of my memories

of it.

While I'm here

Did I ever tell you

I was once unreasoned out of existence?

it felt good to be free

and then you brought me back
why,

I don't know
I don't care

I forgot to tell you

my memory would have been fine
without you.

I needed the room anyways.

The dead god goes camping

She tries to park her SUV into the sky
she says there's a spot between the trees
and gets angry because SUVs don't fly

and then she laughs like a crazy woman
zips up

SUV,
where she left it

She points through trees saying,
there's water in-between them,
if we had canoes we could get there

she folds promises on her knees and says,
drowning only takes one syllable to die,
but it's quiet *and sleeping is nice here.*

Muse's standard contract(s)

I'm taking it as it is I'm taking it as it is because it's
taken too long to get myself here

I can take it as it is because its taken me   a lot of me
from one side of it's ugly mouth to

the other, spit me-out covered in it's mouth-cum
here I can take it

hear I can take it there I can't take it   and stay the fuck
out of my brain   I can't take it

I tried to take it   but I just so tried   and   empty
inside   *is this it?*   I must be made

of holes and some kind of music   this is why drinking
and smoking and petting the cat

are so easy   I am holes   water is holes   cat are holes
I can take nothing   only feel it

If we are holes then you could live through me
I could live through you   we could be

living together   our lives.

Margaret Atwood's library

last night I dreamed I was in Margaret Atwood's library

I was *Surfacing* the isles

stealing what I could carry,

and because she was really a witch she caught me
and threw *Lady Oracle(s)* at me,

they bounced off, causing no *Bodily Harm*.

I said back off bitch, these are mine books now

to read, and to smell, and to dream

and have them stolen from me in a dream

where words are curses and

images are pondered.

and I write(d) till I wake(d)

all *Oryx and Crake(d)*.

Whatever a Killdeer stands up to see

The bird I caught as a child
I let go as an old man

it ran away
like it had just been born.

I looked at my hands,
small, and empty as the sky.

Cygnus punch

I want to write poems
about you

feeding me peaches

warm and ripe

end of summer on
your finger
my tongue wetting both,

peach juice dripping down the sky.

The Douglas, Walt Whitman circa 1967

There is a man that lives in Douglas, ON
that looks like Walt Whitman,
who?
gave up on wood and the world long ago,
got himself a pick-up truck,
found himself a dog

or, a dog found him
licked him and said,

I am Walt Whitman,
who tells me,

as he tells you

Walt Whitman,
who are you?

Always propagandas

Mankind's last radio signals weaved through the air,
in the end, *listening,* not even Moscow was there

so too, that mighty king,
Beijing
was wiped away, that day,

we thought it was the sun,

I can't tell who fired first, that fateful
burst from hell, even Washington, stood no chance,
I stood and watched, the president piss his pants.

It's all gone now, and it just as well
anyhow, *reality was always too ridiculous*
to be believed.

Also by David Groulx

- *The Windigo Chronicles*

- *Rising with a Distant Dawn*

- *Imagine Mercy*

- *From Turtle Island to Gaza*

- *Under God's Pale Bones*

- *Wabigoon River Poems*

- *These Threads Become a Thinner Light*

- *In the Silhouette of Your Silences*

- *When Angels Slept on Steel*

- *The Long Dance*

www.ingramcontent.com/pod-product-compliance
Lightning Source LLC
LaVergne TN
LVHW051219070526
838200LV00064B/4975